Out of Place

Out of Place

Poems by Eli Mandel
Preface and Photographs by Ann Mandel

Porcepic urges educators and institutions to refrain from photocopying parts of books for class distribution. This book has been designed in a low-cost edition and royalties are paid to the author. Purchase of all copies required is the appropriate method of distribution to ensure fair recompense.

(Discounts are available on bulk orders.)

Cover design by Catherine Wilson.
Printed and bound in Canada by the Hunter Rose Company.

77 78 79 80 81   5 4 3 2 1

Distribution:

CANADA
Burns & MacEachern Ltd.
62 Railside Road
Don Mills, Ontario
M3A 1A6

U.S.A.
Press Porcepic Ltd.
70 Main Street
Erin, Ontario
N0B 1T0

U.K. & EUROPE
Books Canada Ltd.
1 Bedford Road
London N2
England

Canadian Shared Cataloguing Publication Data

Mandel, Eli, 1922—
   Out of Place

ISBN 0-88878-074-5 bd.   ISBN 0-88878-075-3 pa.

I. Title.

PS8526.A49088   C811'.5'4   C77-001117-9
PR9199.3.M36088

'Badland country,' Israel thought. . . . It didn't look like badland country to him, yet the whole of the southern border from Roch Percée east of Hirsch to Shaunavon, over 200 miles west, was called badland country. . . .

Land of Hope by Clara Hoffer
and F.H. Kahan

"Artifacts Near Long Creek"

From official records it is learned that at various times in the past, bones of human beings have been uncovered in the same general area but all at higher prairie levels. These are not the products of prehistoric times. They are the remains of white men, trappers, wayfarers or even bad men fleeing from capture, whose bodies were interred just where they died.

Estevan The Power Centre by Andrew King

the nature of fiction
supposes our presence

preface:

Knowing we could not take those papers from the
vault, yet curious to know their contents, we moved
into it and settled down for whatever stay seemed
necessary. What pages we were not reading and sorting
served for mattresses, sheets, and head rests.
When we decided a page was insignificant for our
purposes or saw it was blank we placed it in a
pile to use for wiping ourselves or for after love.
Others became serviettes, sunshades, etc.

Crackers, cheese, Fresca, we brought from the car
and settled down to work. At first we could make
no sense of things, and I spent long hours staring
from the black interior to the blazing doorway.
When my eyes burned past that white rectangle, I
could see long beige and yellow prairie grasses,
air so bright small star-motes swam in its atmosphere,
like when you knuckle in your eyelids then open them
fast. Beyond that a gravel road paling along the
curve of a hill. I knew the grain elevator was to
the right but refused to lean forward to see, leaving
the framed picture intact. Bringing my sight back
into the room required another period of blindness
before the layered white paper emerged from the dark.
Then colour, a greyness, reappeared, and the corners
of the cement vault.

Our work proceeded over days. Some papers were
clearly accounts, farm machinery bills, shipping
invoices, feed allotments, egg sales' receipts,
storage charges from the elevators. Others concerned
religious matters, the finances of the congregation,
salary of the rabbi, attempts to finance a visiting
cantor. We assembled all these as chronologically
as we could. There were also pages torn from old
magazines, including covers from the earliest Life
issues, a slim Queen Elizabeth (now Queen Mother)
in ball gown, tiara, and marcelled hair, another of
Toscanini playing piano with his granddaughter.

Some pages did not seem to fit anywhere, seemed to
be a diary or fiction of a kind, printed professionally
yet appearing never to have been bound. Not numbered.
And containing, we came to see, local place names,
references to this colony, this farm, even to this
vault. Using sentence structure from bottom and
top lines, we put the sheets together in what we
conceived was the right order, then began to read.

The dark slid over our shoulders as we read
sitting cross-legged facing the bright doorway.
A peculiar tale emerged, the pilgrimage west of
a man and wife from the east to the place of his
birth, home of his ancestors, a search for a
lost home. Evidently the place they came to was
this farm. The account of their journey often
moved us, perhaps because we understood so
clearly what ruined heritage they must have
discovered, the abandoned house, rusting bedspring,
stove weathering in tall dry grass, one spare
tilting door jamb framing more prairie only, and
this doorless vault open to wind, cold, heat,
insects. The last pages were missing but we could
see the end. We put down the story and turned back
toward the vault.

I
The Return

the return:

        in the estevan poem, for example,
        how everyone can be seen eating
        or is it reading
                  but not everyone
        there is myself in the souris valley
        forty years later
                Ann
        looking at wild flowers
        cactus   their thick colours

        I remember how I dreamt
        her
           pale as a flower
           in the white sun
        and in the dream
        she is taking pictures

        she photographs me
        walking away
        along a curving path
        the flowers coloured

                and
        my father appears
        my mother appears
        saying no words
        troubled
                and all
        the ghostly jews
        of estevan
                praying
        in the synagogue
          of the valley
        in the covenant
          of coal mines
        in these pictures
          of estevan

and omens   windows
facing inward
                    "an ideal
inserted into the plane
we call reality"   words
warning this is the place
you reach
              to name
remember and recite

the Hebrew alphabet
Invictus the first three
lines of Genesis
the unremembered man who stole
children from an empty town and
Latin   heroes in the hills and
glyphs uncles cousins step-
grandfather's sons and sisters

whatever has been hidden here
remains of speech
                          the town lives
in its syntax we are ghosts

look   on the road beyond
mesas and moonscape
hoodoos   signs cut in rock
graffiti   gods
an indescribable border

doors of perception:

roads lead here   there
on the prairie Ann holds the Pinto
along great swoops of highway down
from Lloydminster past Batoche
rebellion Rudy's book researched
prophetic voices as a guide

in Huxley's version time curves
upon itself
            cities of the mescal dream
turned biblical   jeweled places
palaces of John in Revelation
Blake's engraving the drunkenness
of Smart's madness   prophecy

our history is in motion   curved
like straight correction lines
earth-measured on a western grid
place known through time   time
measuring place
                Thompson walked
through unafraid for knowing
measurement and lore
                    ignorant
of clocks and vision we accelerate
a sweep through dying towns and farms

now is the badlands   measure
our choices random we believe
whatever we can find or where the map
of our own voices leads us listening to

the road to the cancer clinic
past the sundial's didacticism
toward the language of shadows
bedlam the alcoholic's nightmare
uses of wheat and rye and mould

strict farms die
beside the rails the roads
the sons construct
the rules of mind

the jewish exodus from shtetl to the plains
leads to this eygpt abraham learned
dream-sickness and the way to heal
a place of bread and chemistry

madness is neither east nor north
Riel was hung in streets
I walked on every day to school

Note: Abraham Hoffer, son of Israel, is mentioned in a footnote to Huxley's *Doors of Perception and Heaven and Hell*. A psychiatrist, Abraham Hoffer has done pioneer work in the uses of lysergic acid as a means of exploring the nature and causes of schizophrenia and alcoholism. His father was a wheat farmer.

birthmark:

seeing a mouse
my mother struck her temple

he'll be marked at birth
she said
        the women cried

I carry the souris
on my brow
        the river
in my head
        the valley
of my dreams
still echoes
with her cry

souris river:

the mouse runs through passover and the harvest of matzoh
in its muddy layers of saying spread in the valley
joseph-dreams   thin years of wind storms
jews fleeing   fat years for egyptians

it is the blade of yom kippur unyielding
book of years
                        it runs through the province of poetry
                        it speaks in the barred hebrew syntax
                        "wayfarers ... fleeing from capture"

jewish river where my boyhood drowned
harvests of coal and desire
                        "not the products of prehistoric times"

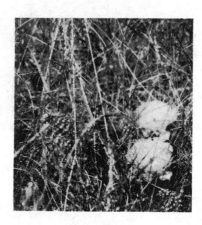

18

badlands:

1

black against sky
four horses   simple
particulars   amid
the endless treachery
that is remembering

there are no definitions

2

neither difficult nor easy
crossings
            happen
it appears

3

understand this
simplicity
this land is
treacherous

between Hirsch and
Hoffer
            it is
plain

4

neither difficult nor easy
crossings
                appear
it happens

5

four horses   amid
the endless treachery
that is remembering

desire

near Hirsch a Jewish cemetery:

> ann is taking pictures again
> while I stand in the uncut grass
> counting the graves: there are forty
> I think
>   the Hebrew puzzles me
> the wind moving the grass
> over the still houses of the dead
>
> from the road a muffled occasional
> roar   cars passing   no one there
> casts a glance at the stone trees
> the unliving forest of Hebrew graves
>
> in the picture I stand arms outstretched
> as if waiting for someone
>   I am
> in front of the gates you can see
> the wind here   the grass
> always bending the stone unmoved

rabbi berner's farm:

        record our searching for the place
        the years of childhood blown across
        has scattered like the jews of Hirsch
        wherever secondary highways lead
        through renewed green fields roads
        passing cattle sheds
                his first wife
        one son   friends   inhabit   land lying
        here or close to other townships
        of the dead   he is alone
        an island now
        under warm rains and cedar

        not even ruins here

slaughterhouse:

after the morning in the slaughterhouse
grandfather leading me back to the kitchen
the farm unpainted weathered grandmother
milking guts of shit for skins and kishke
it's not a place for boys she says
her face redder than strawberries
her hands like cream

lost place:

in the book of years
berner told me could be found
your own name exactly spelled
his own his sons the russian
names of villages and jews

twelve strangled ducklings
laughter in bed

you were written

I read the land for records now

wild strawberries   cocoa-butter
taste of Hirsch
                        bags of curdling
warm spent streams

tested on a hair of berner's beard
the ritual slaughter knife

even the blood has disappeared

STRIKE   sept 1931:

the coal miners stand in groups their faces like
Al Jolson's in Sonny Boy/they raise fists toward the
Chief of Police/he is wearing a blue uniform with
brass buttons on the jacket the red town hall at
his back and behind it the black water tower/the
siren at the top of the tower is blowing although it
isn't noon

the coal miners stand in groups their faces like
Al Jolson's in Sonny Boy/a woman in a long dress
raises both arms/she is shouting beside a touring
sedan/the Mounted Police come round the corner
on foot/they are dressed in brown jackets with Sam
Browne belts and brown trousers with a long yellow
stripe down the leg/they carry their pistols at
eye level

the coal miners run this way and that/one is falling
there is smoke around the guns of the Mounted Police/
windows are breaking/stones fly through the windows/
a coal miner with a face like Al Jolson's in Sonny
Boy is shouting

Musical Estevan

"Many a long winter night was made pleasurable when
neighbours would gather in some home and heartily
join in the singing of old favourite songs, even without
a solitary instrument to maintain a good intonation."

Estevan The Power Centre

26

bienfait july 1/74:

there is no content: except
a fat man in blue overalls
sitting beside a 7-up cooler
in the fourth store across a line
light moving back and forth defines

avoid heroism and gods
nearby in stone
past moonscape and river
they are not yours

no one has the right to memories
in the sun I see my father falling
guns blossom my red-bearded Hebrew
teacher slashes my knuckles for a thought
I think of English poetry the text
mysterious his children carrying
miners and policemen to the library
as the spine carries the silver cord
precious fluid for the golden bowl

aesthetics answers to our need
for structures in our sweat   tender
the copies of Tarzan/lovely
the book of mars
                        turn southward
there the badlands lie

estevan, 1934:

            remembering the family we
            called breeds   the Roques
            their house smelling of urine
            my mother's prayers before
            the dried fish she cursed
            them for their dirtiness their
            women I remember too
                                    how
            seldom they spoke and
            they touched one another

            even when the sun killed
            cattle and rabbis
                        even
            in poisoned slow air
            like hunters
                    like lizards
            they touched   stone
            they touched
                    earth

lines for an imaginary cenotaph:

george hollingdale
bruce carey
george chapman
jacob barney mandel

William Tell Mandel: sd
Capt A.W. (ab) Hardy

Isaac Berner
                    Annie's
son

all the kinds of war
we say our kaddish for

chief Dan Kennedy
singing
beneath the petroglyphs
hoodoos we sd
at Roch Percée

Assiniboine songs

returning from war:

           (for jbm 1918-1944)

       floors gleaming in the white frame house
       yellow as wax the night before he died
       she said her eyes yellow as a hawk's
       she saw him dressed in white   clean
       she said this in the room   the blinds
       drawn   heat leaning on the house
       over the room's dusk the floor's gleam
       white   he was so clean

       in the estevan summer
       hazardous as desert hear
       gopher squeaks momentary hawks
       lean in the pushing and shoving
       wind   the sun breathing
heat
          and the impossibility of death

Recognition Names:

Mrs. C. Boakes, T.A. Perry, W.A. Ellis, H. Nicholson,
W.W. Lynd QC, Miss Nora Mather, D.A. Bannatyne, Greg Trout,
Mrs. Carl Anderson, Mrs. David Bannatyne Sr., C.D. Griffith,
George Lawrence, Carl Skoberg, A.C. Bannatyne, M.L.
Clenndennan, A. W. Forgay, W.J. Rupert, Stan Mays,
Ken Johns.

Estevan The Power Centre

petroglyphs at st victor:

1

watching the sun
watching the sun's wheel
great slow metaphors
wheel toward me out of the sun

they take my eyes from my head
they place my eyes on rocks
they take my crying tongue
they wheel back toward the sun
their black hands carrying my name

now my drawings of god
look no better than my child's
drawing of me
     I remember
the sun his arms flailing
wheat and skin his mouth
warning of hollows and gulleys
one eye grinning news
about crossings
      I try feet now
get the toes wrong
forget the signals once again

whether the snake's head
points inside or outside the sun
for circling the snake ridge

I've always been wrong
about metaphors
about the five figures
of discourse
      the seventy
names of rhetoric and tree
alphabets
     when they gave me
my name I knew the only one
to follow me would mistake
my image/sign
      all the others
praising the gods

33

2

the crooked gods:

    do they mean anything?
    I ask Ann
         parkland
    rolling below sandstone

    silent
        she turns
    the camera
         here
    there
       I kneel
    before the crooked gods

    last light wheeling
    over the land
    their handprints
    their great feet
    their stone faces
    move
        turning
    we leave
    take with us
    photographs
    silent
       as
    their open mouths

3

below the petroglyphs
separate as Quebec
St Victor maintains
direction
          in badlands
four horses on a hill
become a black turmoil
scattered gravel on a road
somersaulting birds
another god
hangs on his cross
near Gravelbourg

we drive through names:
Coronach Canopus Constance
Big Beaver Hart Ceylon Glasnevin
Ogema Horizon Assiniboia
La Fleche McCord Mankota
Stonehenge Montagu
Readlyn Willow Bunch
Dahindel Wheatstone Crystal Hill
Galilee Truax Amulet
Pangman Khedive
          until

Point Alison
where the super-continental stands
our children crying out
barely glimpse redness a form
the end of names and aesthetics

later
amid wreckage of slippers
licorice I remember the cut
god's mouths at Wood Mountain
rhetoric of stone its bluntness

Ann
talking
about children
tomorrow
our return
home
train time

647 Maple Dr.
Weyburn, Sask.,
April 7, 1975

Prof. Eli Mandel,
English Dept.
York University,
Toronto, Ont.

Dear Professor Mandel,

Heard you on 'This Country in the Morning' and was
more than surprised when you mentioned that your new
book on Poetry and Prose will be about the ghost
Jewish Colony of Hoffer (or Sonnenfeld Colony which is
the correct name).

Whereas my husband and I were both born in the colony
and are still carrying on farming operations there and have
a great interest in that area we were wondering where you
got your information.

It was interesting to hear you say that your wife
has been out taking pictures. Would it be possible
to know of this, and when and where do you plan to have
your book published. We would like to buy it when it
becomes available.

Thank you.

Yours truly.

Mrs. N. Feldman

sonnenfeld:

Mrs. Feldman writes to tell me
I've got the ghosts wrong

it isn't Hoffer, she says,

I look again
at our photographs
fading pastels
grainy texture

as if it happened
long ago
          Mrs. Feldman
I say to myself softly
I can't see you in the picture
there is no one there

were we in the wrong place?
who is mistaken?
what can the letter possibly mean
its words in pale blue ink
copied carefully as a will
or a schoolteacher's correction
of a bad essay
on the geography of the west?

the hoffer colony:

just as in McCourt's *Saskatchewan*
though unlike his prose
clapboard buildings on a ridge
pastel fields tree stumps
an overturned quebec heater
iron bedstead rusting
useless springs
                    the clichés
appalling   over-written
like a bad travel book

and in a concrete vault its floor
littered with prairie I find
scripture a farmer's exodus Israel
Hoffer's accounting I begin
to feel gloomy about possibilities
in mythology some books of the bible
devote themselves to family lines
some to a census
                        there are stories
about passionate heroic tax
collectors   others where merchants
ruined by investment sell children

I look uneasily at grain inventories
machinery bills, newspapers
think about my uncle standing
among rocks with Israel
both Jews proud and successful

before we take our easy leave
how should we understand
prophecies and miracles?

sponsors names:

W.W. Lynd, H. Nicholson, Mrs. Ida Peterson,
Phillips Family, Paul Grundeen, Ronald Galloway,
Mrs. D.L. Irvine, Mrs. W. Henneberg, David A. Bannatyne,
Donald Perry, George Greene, Frank Mather, Everet
Murphy, Clifford Holmgren

Estevan The Power Centre

Last of the Buffalo   *The Soo Line*

Mandel Henry prop.
M Mandel and Co h 938 Second St.

II
The Double

the doppelganger:

ways to prevent me:

refusing to be interrupted especially by children
single-mindedness to the point of brutality
in all matters of politics religion metaphysics &
the character and lives of your closest friends
praising the worst lines of your fellow writers
jogging followed by volley ball and cold showers
concentrated masturbation before and after sex
sleeping with a towel knotted in your back
inspired teaching ferocious tactics in rumoli
combinations of alcohol librium and   bad novels

seeing I'm here you know all methods fail
you don't even know how long it has been
what I might have said to children or others
now it's forever too late
no one could possibly know
you've been gone for days
when I make love to your wife
she will moan and praise you
asking you never to leave

where shall I say you have gone?

the doppelganger (2):

think about changes
the calendar of your bones
page after page of skin
lifted from your days
and darkness drifting on the earth
across the rim of turn
your metamorphosis from sperm
the sperm's anxieties
the foetal journey
through waves of mother
urging in her self a self
through coursing blood
in which you swam
whatever fish you were
this is no longer you:
I take possession of your eyes
to see the mother in your blood

new politics of blood are born
the journey in your bones begins
again: here is the day you could not know

doubles: estevan

1

the Orpheum shows a desert film
in Ann's picture the Orpheum is pale
against a paler sunlight a washed-out
film: someone who could be me stands
beside a sweet shop that the Mathers ran
for boys whose faces had been ruined

on such illusions we have built our lives
palaces of art where Sara dreams
her precious dream of being
                                        all that
every image makes impossible and true

licorice whips and jawbreakers
that sweetness of the tongue mocks
broken faces of the ones returned
like images of films we fled
the hunchback lobster monster
broken patched
                    I stand
inside the film and stare
at places that I never knew

2

pictures
          in the baptist tent
          of jesus who stared
          at you

          in the chatauqua
          of mary who smiled
          at you

          in The Estevan Mercury
          window of ladies who
          became a skull
          and smiled
          at you

          unholy places
          the churches of estevan

3

in the photograph of the Orpheum
the marquee lettering says Devils Island Air Conditioned
Comfort slant sunlight marking off plaster abstracts beside
Mather's Candy Store and you can see me standing near the
store where looking for jawbreakers and licorice whips
before the Saturday afternoon show I watched for three
deformities and later heard the ventroloquist's spitting
dummy speak thinking of buggery somewhere in that store
though it may have been inside a school not
even mentioned in the book of Estevan and it was long
ago anyway.

the cause of doubles:

on the way to the faculty club
you pass a zone through which neutrons flow
through you through trees through wives
through walls of brick or
hangings in the club
                            on one side you
are you/on the other you yourself but new
a kind of Paul upon the road to the
Alberta faculty club
                                this new one
lectures in your voice but transforms
                                                you
before you cross the zone/think:
it might be chemicals or breakfast food
a hair spray used unthinkingly
before you crossed the zone

but now like David Bowie in the film
he's falling in/the other you takes off
his eyes it isn't cancer after all
it isn't what you thought it was
beside yourself you think
of gifts
            Houdini in his chains
his silk-lined coffin the undead
Doc Savage poet madly writing praise
to god in bedlam transforming seas
to bring him coral bones and pearls
the other you speaks of
                                    you
cross the zone
                        later
warn your puzzled friends
of breakfast food and sprays

questions a double asks:

whether anything in your dreams accounts for his
    appearing now
how it is the explanation of acute anxiety does not
    suffice to dispel him
what in your philosophical readings could be consistent
    with the notion of reduplication
whether he is a refutation of clock time and a way
    to justify eternity
why you are afraid of him as shown by your blood
    pressure and pulse

does his appearance improve your sexual performance
has the government of Canada Ontario Alberta significantly
    improved because of his presence
what explanations you offer to your father/to your department
    chairman/to the department of revenue
give a detailed account of all sado-masochistic
    fantasies you entertain
refer to each scatalogical childhood incident
    coprophilia necrophilia sodomy

do you know yourself

have you any reason for hope or delight

why do you think I am here

will you change your life

account for the difference between the spider and
    the spider plant

have you considered the fern the coleus the philodendron
    the patience plant the flowers the hoya the lilies
    of the day the ants bees sweetness light the sun the
    moon

why are you writing out these questions

will you do nothing to help me

is poetry all you have to offer

the double world:

       it is variously believed that this world is the
double of another, as in Plato, Swedenborg, Malebranche,
some of Immanuel Kant, Arthur C. Clarke, Isaac Asimov,
Stanley Kubrick
                  Two clocks set at the same time in
identical universes should stop at the same time.
This clock is a shadow of that real clock. When I
look at my clock I have no way of knowing whether I am in
the first or second universe. It is spring there too:
and the other Ann has grown an avocado exactly the same
height, greenness, number of leaves as the one Ann grew
here or there. My grandfather Berner weighed the same
in both universes, sang sweet Jewish psalms, ate sour
curds. In the two graveyards Annie Berner is dead.
Nothing on either prairie changes though the winds blow
across immensities your heart would shrivel to imagine
knowing they pass between the worlds and can be heard to do
so on the road to Wood Mountain. That is what was written
in the rocks.

instructions:
(on the nature of doubles and doubling)

all mirrors should be covered
do not look deeply into a sink of hot water
ditto cold
wear rings on only two fingers
your eyes are doubles doubled
everything divides by two or is uneven
poetry consists in the doubling of words
doubled words are poetic words
this is the true meaning of duplicity
each poem speaks to another poem
the language of poetry is a secret language
these are the true doubles

false doubles are ones and threes
four is a good number

doubled names are : eli   elijah
                     jesse   jesus
                     paul   saul
                     joseph   pharoah
                                    etc.

in Hebrew this is common
no one knows the jewish name of god

indian names are secret
poetry is the naming of secret names
among these are:

           god
           spirit
           alphabets

           names in stone
           doubled names
           the psalms
           hoodoos
           animals
           eyes
           jewels

the place of no shadows called badlands
the place of shadows called badlands
you begin to see the difficulties

various kinds of doubles:

Mirrors Rivers Water Wells
Jewels Babies Twins
Actors Brothers Sisters
Fathers Mothers Sons
Daughters Lovers Others
Princes Swans Frogs
Maidens Cousins Others

Plastic Neon Glass
Gold Silver Rings
Diamond Earrings
Ringing Dancing Drowning
Eating Dolls Rabbits
Thin Men Fat Men   Tattoos
Giants Heroes Roots
Gardens Mandrake Mermaids
Helen Paul Saul
Clever Odysseus
David and Jonathan
Crickets Locusts Gophers
Kings Queens Jacks
Shadows and Rainbows
Stars Suns Moons
Sundogs Barking
White Hopes Black Men
Beulah Couples
Writing
Pictures
Huck Finn
Tom Sawyer
Mark Twain

Others

various kinds of doubles:

Mirrors Rivers Water Wells
Jewels Babies Twins
Actors Brothers Sisters
Fathers Mothers Sons
Daughters Lovers Others
Princes Swans Frogs
Maidens Cousins Others

Plastic Neon Glass
Gold Silver Rings
Diamond Earrings
Ringing Dancing Drowning
Eating Dolls Rabbits
Thin Men Fat Men   Tattoos
Giants Heroes Roots
Gardens Mandrake Mermaids
Helen Paul Saul
Clever Odysseus
David and Jonathan
Crickets Locusts Gophers
Kings Queens Jacks
Shadows and Rainbows
Stars Suns Moons
Sundogs Barking
White Hopes Black Men
Beulah Couples
Writing
Pictures
Huck Finn
Tom Sawyer
Mark Twain

Others

III
A Suite for Ann

Fear of Flying

I dream of flying but I fear
I either will or will not fly
or flying will not land or will
or landing will at once arise

waking
            I place my feet on
creaky floors
                              you beside me
dream of stairs   climbing
vines
            and wings

Strange Places

the places that we go are strange
but stranger that we go to place
our strangeness where we neither
know we were nor where but only
that the place we know is neither

but the way that tells us
we have been
                    not only here
but where there was the telling

it was so
            we did not choose it
it was
        so

Place

a line
colour

history
places
          never
choose
never
          it is
we know
love
          not
chosen

here

The Wayfarer

Darkness flows over the green
the horn fills with night

languid
where children are laughing

though she sings of night
she remembers
                    journeys

look how thick the forest
where she has been
or where
              night
spills over

IV
Epilogue

on the political problem of writing a regional poem
jewish rural historical nostalgic:

for rick salutin

stupidity is the devil. Look in the eye of a chicken and you'll know. It's the
most horrifying, cannabalistic and nightmarish creature in this world.
—Werner Herzog

On Fridays in Regina the difficulties become acute, how to
smuggle two live chickens in a burlap sack down the street
of Ukrainian neighbours, past two alien churches, one Russian
Orthodox, its onion domes looming over me (alien afraid as
Klein would say) like a Chagall version of shtetl-life, the
other Greek, its angular priestly spire aloofly critical
of the gross yiddishkeit of chickens. Their obstinacy, their
cunning. How do they manage to wiggle their obscene squawking
heads through burlap? Why should my fate be set by fowl?
The murderous notions in my head on Friday, Sabbath eve:
"chicken you'll die before the ritual blessing, that's for sure",
detestable the squalid hut to which I move, its bloody
rows of funnels, feathers stuck to crusted blood of slaughtered
birds.

I think of god, his commandments regulating the sanctity
of chicken soup, appeal the case to high authority. "It isn't
fair" I say. "To whom" my grandfather's omnipotent
reply, "you or the chickens?"

My radical jewish friend, the dramatist, having celebrated
the revolutionary spirit of Anglo-Canadian farmers, explains,
his pale blue eyes ablaze with lust or hate or warming to
his task:
        BOURGEOISE PREJUDICE ISRAELI EXPANSIONISM JEWISH
        PLOTS VULGARITY EXPLOITATION SORDID JEWISH
        WRITING SELLING JEWISHNESS LANDLORDS JEWISH
        LANDLORDS FUNDS TO ZIONISM

America, my enemy. America, what have you done to us? To
our alliance with the true proletariat? The vision possesses
me of the workers of Kitimat marching to free the boys of Regina
from the tyranny of chicken soup. I must rid myself of
deviationism. The possibility of humiliating chickens and
schochets, the excitement of the Cultural Revolution, Red Guards
descending on regional theatres, slaughtering playwrights.

Meanwhile the chickens continue to squawk, past Eleventh Avenue,
down the mean streets, St John, Halifax, Montreal, Toronto,
Ottawa, to where the gleaming razor waits. I hear the ritual
muttered prayer, a whisper faster than the slit of knife
over plucked throats, blood draining into funnels. Later,
the salted, watered birds steaming in their soup adorn
our place, the unpolitical whiteness of the table-cloth,
familial statements of poor silver-plate and hand-worked
candle-sticks, historical re-enactments of a pledge, the
wedding of the sabbath day, dressed, proud, adorned we
celebrate.

Across the nation jewish dramatists recite the commune's
words. I see my mother and my father clubbed to death.
Cheated, I wish these ghost poems dead or burned
but put them in this book.

The commissars have won again.

Jewish Colonization Association

jn/fg

46, Queen Anne's Gate,
London, SW1H 9AP.
13th July 1976.

Hon. Alvin Hamilton, P.C., M.P.
House of Commons,
Ottawa.

Dear Mr. Hamilton,

Jewish cemetery near Hirsch, Saskatchewan

I thank you for your letter of 28th June containing
a very interesting suggestion concerning the marking and
maintenance in perpetuity of the old Jewish cemetery which
served the original settlement which we called Hirsch Colony.

The problem is well known to us and we have been
considering how it might best be solved, since we have had
other suggestions besides yours. We intend to adopt a solu-
tion as satisfactory as possible to all the interested parties.

I will not fail to keep you informed.

Yours sincerely,

Joseph Nialle

Director.

PICTURES IN AN INSTITUTION

1

Notice: all mirrors will be covered
                 the mailman is forbidden to speak
                 professors are confined to their offices
                 faculties no longer exist.

2

I speak of what I know,
how uncle Asher, spittle on his lips,
first typed with harvest hands the fox
across a fence and showing all good men
come to their country's aid rushed off to Israel
there to brutalize his wife and son

how step-grandfather Barak wiped
sour curds out of his curly beard
before he roared the Sabbath in my ears
what Sara, long his widow, dreamed
the night she cried: God, let him die at last,
thinking perhaps of Josef who had lost
jewels in Russia where the Cossack rode
but coughed his stomach out in Winnipeg

Your boredom does not matter. I take,
brutal to my thoughts, these lives, defy
your taste in metaphor; the wind-break
on the farm that Barak plowed to dust
makes images would ruin public poetry.

The rites of love I knew:
how father cheated brother, uncle, son,
and bankrupt-grocer, that we might eat
wrote doggerel verse, later took his wife,
my mother, in the English way beside my bed.
Why would he put his Jewishness aside?
Because there was no bread?
                        Or out of spite
that doctors sliced his double rupture,
fingered spleen, and healed his bowel's ache?

Lovers lie down in glades, are glad.
These, now in graves, their headstones sunk,
knew nothing of such marvels, only God, his ways,
owning no texts of Greek or anthropology.

3

Notice: the library is closed to all who read
                 any student carrying a gun
                 registers first, exempt from fines,
                 is given thirteen books per month,
                 one course in science, one in math,
                 two options
                              campus police
                 will see to co-ed's underwear

4

These names I rehearse:
                      Eva, Isaac,
Charley, Yetta, Max
                 now dead
or dying or beyond my lies

till I reeling with messages
and sick to hold again their bitter lives
put them, with shame, into my poetry.

5

Notice: there will be no further communication
                 lectures are cancelled
                 all students are expelled
                 the reading of poetry is declared a public
                                                      crime

Acknowledgements

This poem records a series of journeys. It is fiction not fact
though it originates in an attempt to give some form to
experiences ranging from a return to the country of the poem
to memories and rumours about the past, especially stories told
me of the Jewish settlement of southern Saskatchewan in the
late years of the 19th century and the early years of the
20th, stories yet to be told in their true and full dimension,
heroic tales. Nothing in Jewish lore of which I am aware justifies
my version of spirits and ghosts in the poem. But there are Jewish
stories of dybbuks and the golem. The companion and guide is
of course a familiar figure in tales of journeys. Estevan, Hirsch,
Hoffer, my grandparents, their friends, farms, homes, and people
I knew and know here inhabit fantasies that are my own, as
Mrs. Feldman's letter indicates.

I am grateful to all those whose remarks and comments provided
direction, to the Canada Council for grants in aid of research
and travel, to the Ontario Arts Council for support, to Henry
Mandel who led me to valuable sources, and above all to Ann, for
whom this book was written.

Certain passages have been quoted from *Land of Hope, Estevan The
Power Centre* and *The Soo Line*. "Estevan 1934" and "Pictures
in an Institution" appeared in *Crusoe* and separately in *Stony Plain*
and *An Idiot Joy*. Acknowledgements as well are due to *Twelve Prairie
Poets, Modern Canadian Poetry*, and *15 Canadian Poets*.

Table of Contents

Books by Eli Mandel

Trio (with Phyllis Webb and Gael Turnbull) 1954
Fuseli Poems 1960
Poetry 62 — Ed. with Jean Guy Pilon — 1962
Black and Secret Man 1964
Criticism: The Silent Speaking Words 1966
An Idiot Joy 1967
Irving Layton 1969
Five Modern Canadian Poets — Ed. 1971
Contexts of Canadian Criticism — Ed. 1971
Poets of Contemporary Canada —Ed. 1972
Eight More Canadian Poets — Ed. with Ann Mandel — 1972
English Poets of the Twentieth Century — Ed. with Des Maxwell — 1972
Crusoe 1973
Stony Plain 1973
Another Time 1977
Out of Place 1977